Stuart was born in Berkshire, England in 1986 and moved to Perth, Western Australia in 1988 where he still resides today. He cherishes spending time with his son of whom he is extremely proud. Stuart started writing as a way of expressing himself and began penning poetry when he was in his early teens.

This is dedicated to my late father, Richard, whose words of wisdom and advice still echo through my mind to encourage me to be the best version of myself.

Stuart Turnbull

ENTER THE DARKNESS

AUSTIN MACAULEY PUBLISHERS™
LONDON • CAMBRIDGE • NEW YORK • SHARJAH

Copyright © Stuart Turnbull 2024

The right of Stuart Turnbull to be identified as author of this work has been asserted by the author in accordance with sections 77 and 78 of the Copyright, Designs and Patents Act 1988.

All rights reserved. No part of this publication may be reproduced, stored in a retrieval system, or transmitted in any form or by any means, electronic, mechanical, photocopying, recording, or otherwise, without the prior permission of the publishers.

Any person who commits any unauthorised act in relation to this publication may be liable to criminal prosecution and civil claims for damages.

This is a work of fiction. Names, characters, businesses, places, events, locales, and incidents are either the products of the author's imagination or used in a fictitious manner. Any resemblance to actual persons, living or dead, or actual events is purely coincidental.

A CIP catalogue record for this title is available from the British Library.

ISBN 9781398476226 (Hardback)
ISBN 9781398476240 (ePub e-book)

www.austinmacauley.com

First Published 2024
Austin Macauley Publishers Ltd®
1 Canada Square
Canary Wharf
London
E14 5AA

Table Of Content

Part 1: First Love   11

  Baby Girl   13

  A Little Bit of Love   14

  I Love   15

Part 2: The Heartache   17

  It Pains Me   19

  Do I Love You?   21

  Love Is Real   22

  No Tears   23

  Soulless   24

  Life   25

  A Life of Sorrow   26

  World Of Fences   29

Part 3: Into the Darkness   31

  The Way I Live   33

  The Horror   35

Cess Pool	*36*
Time To Leave	*37*
Life On the Edge	*38*
Where	*39*
When Will My Number Be Called?	*40*
Inside Of Myself	*42*
Part 4: Glimpses of Light	**45**
Journey	*47*
A Love Learnt	*48*
Guess Who's Back?	*49*
I'm The King	*51*
Part 5: Healing	**55**
Searching For the Day	*57*
Love Me, Love You	*58*
Keep Me	*59*
Alcohol Confidence	*60*
You Wanna Be Me	*61*
I'm Your Best Memory	*63*
Part 6: New Love	**65**
Beauty	*67*
All I Ever Wanted	*68*
Part 7: The Trauma	**69**
Broken	*71*

What Was	*72*
I'm Tired	*73*
Caught Up	*74*
Truth	*75*
In My Mind	*76*
Part 8: Gypsy Girl Encounter	**77**
Gypsy Love	*79*
It Was Over	*80*
The Beast	*81*
Part 9: Back in The Trauma	**83**
The Cycle	*85*
Final Thoughts	*86*

Part 1
First Love

Baby Girl

There is this girl, who I love so dear,
nothing matters whenever she's near,
it's like she's an angel sent from above,
to make me learn all about love.
I love her with all my heart,
So much good about her, where do I start?
She has an amazing personality,
and she cares a lot for humanity.
She's so gorgeous, both inside and out,
She made me realise what relationships are really about.
She makes me feel like I'm the only person in the world,
I feel so special, being around this girl...
She always acts like I'm the only one,
as if it's from me, that the world begun.
With her, I throw all caution to the wind,
because love, is a truly wonderful thing.

A Little Bit of Love

I love the way you smile,
and I love your pretty eyes,
you look at me with style,
or a look of surprise.
Your expressions move my heart,
In a way I don't understand,
But no matter if you're crying or laughing,
I will always be your man.

I Love

I love that sparkle in your eyes,
and I love your sexy thighs.
I love the way you style your hair,
I love everything about you, while you're there.
I love the way that you chose to dress,
and I think it's cute in the way that you stress.
I love it when you tell me how gorgeous you think I am,
baby girl, we go together like Pebbles and Bam-Bam.
We are two of a special kind, never to be separated,
you're like a drug to me, that's why my pupils are always dilated.
When I'm with you, nothing else matters,
but when you're gone, my whole life shatters.
I can't wait for the day that our futures are sealed together.
Coz baby girl, I want us to be together, forever.

Part 2
The Heartache

It Pains Me

It pains me to say,
that I love you still.
It won't go away,
I always will.

For reasons that remain unknown,
I feel as though,
I'm all alone,
with nothing to show.

When we broke up,
My heart broke too.
I've had enough,
of feeling confused and blue.

I keep on going,
but continue to fall down.
With no one showing,
how to turn it all around.

I feel so hollow,
it's like I'm a shell.
Within all the sorrow,
no perception of myself.

I can see the place,
where in death I'll reside.
And I see the face,
that'll be by my side...

Do I Love You?

You ask if I love you,
and if my love is true,
but our love has been betrayed,
it's been betrayed by you.
I was living in the shade,
and I couldn't see the truth,
hoping the rumours would fade,
another diseased youth.

Nothing ever changed,
since you remained the same,
making me deranged,
should have never played your game,
you think that I don't know?
But now I can see,
you're another h*e,
trying to get the best of me.

How many times will you stray?
How many times will I have to catch you?
Before you change your ways?
Is there time to fix you?
Is it all a phase?
Or are you like a statue?
Staying the same until the end of days...

Love Is Real

A love so real,
feelings so deep,
many emotions I feel,
my soul is yours to keep.
Times are hard,
yet, we always carry on,
life, like a glass shard,
yet, we keep each other strong.
More beautiful than life,
more precious than stone,
if you were my wife,
I wouldn't feel alone...

No Tears

No tears are shed,
no sorrow is felt,
the life that you led,
you brought it upon yourself.
A sinful life,
is what you found,
relieve us of strife,
when you're in the ground.

Soulless

A soulless being,
is all you ever were,
too blind, not seeing,
a senseless cur.
The path you chose,
led you nowhere,
but to the rest of those,
in the midst of the devil's stare.

Life

Feeling so numb, because I was too dumb,
too blind to see, what was happening to me.
In way over my head, no more tears to shed,
You took the best of me, no more heart to bleed.
Will it stay the same? Do I yearn for pain?
Being abused and getting used,
getting lied to, why did I let you?
Feeling all alone, no longer in the zone.
At a great cost, and now I'm so lost,
I no longer understand, what it takes to be a man,
feeling worthless, right under the surface.
Trying to be brave, while I feel so afraid.
Where am I going? What should I be doing?
Where do I belong? Where did it all go so wrong?
I've lost too much, and can no longer touch,
why did you stray? And why did I stay?
Where's my Summer in May? Where's my brighter day?
No longer feel alive, God is no longer my guide.
All the visions, and all my missions,
led me to where? They led me here...

A Life of Sorrow

Feeling all alone, in my so-called home,
life unknown, like the garden gnome,
friends aplenty, yet I feel empty,
nothing left to tempt me.

Nothing to gain, in this world of pain,
it's all in vain, when you've been slain,
too much greed in the lives we lead,
bleeding heart since I was a seed.

All the words spoken, just a mere token,
of a life that would never be.
The vision that I had, I must have been mad,
to see what is not for me.

A lost soul, was never my goal,
yet now it's what I am,
when will the bell toll,
for the end of this man.

Has it already rung,
and I did not hear it,
bleeding from the lungs,
and I no longer fear it.

A life that will never be free,
in a world of hurt,
can't you all see,
my heart laying in the dirt.

Deception and lies,
is all I seem to get,
no one hears the cries,
of this worlds' pet.

Everything I do,
and everything I say,
never good enough for you,
so, I try another way.

Still, I never get it right,
because you continue to leave,
another sleepless night,
another day to grieve.

Who is to blame?
Is it you or me?
Is it the flame?
Or is it my destiny?

Destined to be alone,
and to be used,
left on my own,
and still, I get used.

Why do I fall for it?
Each and every time.
falling into the pit,
in my own demise.

World Of Fences

Sweet as honey,
yet hard as stone,
richer than money,
more precious than bone

Your eyes, they glisten,
Like the brightest star.
I will always listen,
wherever you are

Words softly spoken,
Yet wield great power.
Breath a mere token,
Of life as a flower

A smile so proud,
Given with such vehemence.
Tender as a cloud,
With too much lenience

Your smell, so sweet,
Like the freshest air.
But it can't compete,
With you, while you're here.

But now that you're gone,
I have lost all senses.
And I'm all alone,
In a world of fences.

Part 3
Into the Darkness

The Way I Live

I can no longer sleep, coz I'm having some crazy dreams,
It's like I'm in a living nightmare, but I don't hear the screams,
Alcohol doesn't really help me at all anymore,
Yet I still drink, and by the pains, I know I'm getting closer to death's door.
Although I'll admit it, that doesn't really phase me,
Even though I'm getting shown so much love, I just think it's all crazy.
I avoid it all, so I don't get f**ked over again,
And I avoid getting close, I already have friends.

You don't want to see the things I see when I close my eyes,
And you don't want to see any of my life before my demise.
I can guarantee if you even try to walk in my shoes,
Then like me, you'd be crazy too.
I only have love for my closest friends and family,
That way nothing else in this world can fail me,
I utilise everything that God has blesses me with,
And that's why I always feel successful in all that I give.

I don't care if you're jealous of the live that I have,
If you lived your life decently, you'd have no reason to be mad,
I could let you know how it's done, but that's my little secret,
Your messed up life in this world? Damn…you can keep it.
You may wonder how with nightmares and no sleep that my life is so good,
But I feed off the worst of situations, it's like it's my soul's food.

The Horror

So much horror,
And so much pain.
Why do we bother?
When it's all in vain.

Everything you love,
Will be lost.
All for the man above,
But, at what cost?

The world is rampant,
With disease and death.
No longer important,
So I hold my breath.

Things need to change,
Respect needs to be learnt.
I know it sounds strange,
But do you want to be burnt?

Only one life to lead,
Just the one to live.
One colour to bleed,
And one chance to give.

Cess Pool

Living in a cess pool,
so dark and deep.
Quiet now you fool,
the monsters aren't asleep.
In the shadows they lay,
using crevices to hide,
waiting for their prey,
to come where they reside.
You're what they need to survive,
they feed off twisted souls,
a swift death, no need for you alive,
eradicating scum, their only goals.
You should have changed,
when you had your chance,
now the devil has arranged
your soul's deathly dance.

Time To Leave

One life to lead,
one heart to bleed,
I've never had a need,
since I was a seed.
Born to struggle,
is what I was,
heaps of trouble,
chasing a buzz.
It's time to fly,
time to leave,
it's time to fry,
the best of me.

Life On the Edge

One life to live,
one heart to give,
all in pieces,
falling through the sieve.
Coming to bits,
like a broken rock,
life is like nits,
or a broken clock.
Nothing to see,
and nothing to feel,
another being,
cold as steel.
Heart so cold,
cold, like ice,
mind so bold,
Like a rolled dice.
Life is on the edge,
one slip to fall,
pushed through the hedge,
Death to us all.

Where

Where do I go?
Where do I belong?
Nothing left to show,
hear the sorrow in the song.
All the advice,
and there's none for me.
Too much sacrifice,
took the best of me.
Draining away,
in the pain I feel,
turning to clay,
in a world of steel.

When Will My Number Be Called?

Every single day,
I pray to the Lord,
to take me away,
by anything, even the sword.

But, still I am here,
living in the rain.
With death I no longer fear,
just surviving with the pain.

Why must I struggle?
Why must I suffer?
Am I in trouble?
As my life gets rougher.

My pain runs so deep,
it cuts me to my soul.
Is that why I don't sleep?
Is death my only goal?

Is a life of pain my destiny?
Or have I yet to be born?
Waiting for the death of me,
because my soul is torn.

Time is not my healer,
it just brings more hurt.
It's like pains dealer,
until I'm in the dirt.

Inside Of Myself

Deep within my tortured mind,
there's a place I don't wish to find,
a place where the monsters reside,
deep in the darkness is where they hide.
They are the forms of my past demons,
evil beings that don't listen to reason.
Dark beings that I try to ignore,
but they're always knocking at the door.
Occurrences of happenings past,
things that I wished to last,
ultimately turned back on me,
and I was too blind to see,
memories of times that once brought joy,
now bring horror through their evil ploy.
At the time, creating a good memory,
but now these demons make these thoughts my enemy.
At the time we were like bread and butter,
now it's like I'm rich, and you're just gutter.
Deep inside I ignore the sorrow,
Just living for today, not caring for tomorrow.
Although, I can't help but think,
if things were the same now, would I still be tickled pink?

Feelings so great, emotions so pure,
but walked over as if they were manure,
A love so deep, though now a love lost,
gave up a lot of my soul, at a great unjustly cost.

Part 4
Glimpses of Light

Journey

I'm on a journey,
So full of hope.
Avoiding the tourney,
And the lifeless rope.

Prepared for life's challenges,
It's time to meet them head on.
Avoiding all the scavengers,
and the path that I was on.

Seeking life's treasures,
to fill my heart with gold.
Avoiding all the pressures,
and getting old.

Learning priceless knowledge,
so I can become wise.
Avoiding college,
and being asinine when I demise.

Being all I am,
chasing my destiny.
Avoiding all the scams,
and not giving up the best of me.

A Love Learnt

A love once learnt,
a love once lost.
Foundations are burnt,
yet bridges are crossed.

Learning life's lessons,
is not for the light hearted,
Meeting up in sessions,
our thoughts will be chartered.

Discovering something new,
each and every day.
Bite off what you can chew,
don't end up astray.

So much to be found,
many answers do we seek.
Some lost below ground,
too afraid to have a peek.

There's a world to see,
with so much to do.
How do we get free?
Well, that's a lesson for you...

Guess Who's Back?

I'm back in the game,
bigger than ever.
you say it's a shame,
because it was then or never.

I've got money on my mind,
chasing new dreams,
everyday I'm on the grind,
just this one, with no teams.

I have many ways to make that money,
putting it all together,
I think your perception is funny,
coz better than me? It'll be never.

Rolling like a Sherman tank,
I'll be here laughing at you,
all the way to the bank,
because that's what I'm supposed to do.

Only have the one love,
and it's something you'll never know,
I'm at peace like a white dove,
and you're addicted to blow.

I'm back stronger than before,
and I'm living my life,
although it's still a chore,
and I still have strife.

But I'm going to make it,
and you never will,
even if you fake it,
and eat every pill.

I won't slow down,
I won't disappear,
I deserve this crown,
More than anyone here!

I'm The King

Screw the world, coz I'm at the top.
The only one there,
I don't care what you've got, I own the whole shop.
all you can do is stare.

I'm the new king,
you'll never take me down,
all you are a 20-minute fling,
just back up, and don't touch my crown.

People want to see me buried,
coz I live a real good life,
but I am not worried,
only death can defeat me, not your strife.

Love isn't anything but a word,
it doesn't mean a thing to me,
it has become absurd,
but at least I'll always be free.

Pain isn't anything but a phase,
all you have to do is be strong,
because "I love you" is only a phrase,
just hold on, and move on.

It's better to just forget,
don't think of the past,
because all you will get,
is false dreams that never last.

I've seen what I need to see,
seen a world of backstabbing,
I've been where I was meant to be,
to block out all your babbling.

Put up with a lot of lies,
and being cheated on,
by maggots, baby flies,
and that's why I tell you to bring it on.

I live each day as if it were my last,
because I've only got this one life to live,
It's gone so fast, so I no longer dwell on the past,
and I no longer have the need to give.

I proceed to get whatever I want,
just because I can.
I know you're jealous, but don't front,
because I am, the man.
You think that I'm cocky,
but I'm just confident,
I don't care if you block me,
it's because you're jealous, so it's a compliment.

I'm free to do whatever I want to do,
while you just do what you can get away with,
you could have a good life if you wanted to,
but your life is falling through like it's a sieve.

I know my time is running out,
I feel it in my veins,
but I no longer live in a drought,
looking at the world in disdain.

Part 5
Healing

Searching For the Day

I'm eager to find someone that loves and respects herself,
someone that realises, it's love, not money, that's eternal wealth.
I don't care that I'm an old fashioned romantic,
and I don't mind that I live my life so pedantic.
I want to find someone that beams with intelligence,
someone who's like me within my essence,
I cannot wait until the day that we shall meet,
as I know you will forever sweep me off my feet.
Love is the world's greatest emotion,
it knows no boundaries, nor the depths of the ocean.
I can't wait until I receive it unconditionally,
and to receive it for eternity, internally.
I will never let you go,
we were meant to be, and we both know,
true love is my goal, it's my destiny,
and I'll always give you the best of me.
Forever looking forward, to the day we are like one,
and eager for the day, for you to carry our son.
I have high hopes, that he will carry on my legacy,
and I know the words you speak, won't be a fallacy.
Until the day we meet, I'll remain content,
as I know it will be times worth being spent,
because it will all lead to the point where I meet you,
and I'll be happy, as it's what I'm meant to do.

Love Me, Love You

For the feeling of love, I no longer disdain,
because I no longer feel the pain,
even if in 4 days, it would have been 1 year,
I carry on, and once again, love I no longer fear.
I welcome it into my heart, and into my very being,
no longer trying to escape, no longer fleeing.
it's something I am ready, and willing to embrace,
no longer scared by it and trying to save face.
Looking forward to the feelings so warm,
my heart is ready for the emotions to swarm,
no longer treading life with trepidation,
as for what's to come, I've had a premonition.
A love so real, and a love so deep,
a love forever, that lasts til our eternal sleep,
a love so strong it will keep us together, forever,
a love so binding, it will get us through the stormiest weather.

Keep Me

If you have someone that will do anything for you,
keep them.
If you have someone completely devoted to you,
keep them.
If you have someone that's always true,
keep them.
If you have someone that gives you full respect,
keep them.
If you have someone that really knows what love is,
keep them.
If you have someone that wants to have your kids,
keep them.
If you have someone that can't live without you,
keep them.
If you have someone that will do anything to make you happy,
keep them.
If you have someone that will give up anything for you,
keep them.
If you have someone that will do anything to protect you,
keep them.
If you have someone that will die for you,
keep them.

Alcohol Confidence

A litre bottle of Alize and a litre bottle of Jacks,
Now my mind's spinning and all the memories are back,
I don't mind though, it doesn't faze me,
Even when the whole world spins and everything goes hazy,
I have everyone in the world waiting,
Waiting to see me fail because they're all hating,
Because I'm on top of the world, and I ooze confidence,
Even though I love myself, I still love compliments,
They're something I receive every single day,
It makes me cocky as hell, what can I say?
That's why I don't need to wear my jewels,
They already know I'm rich and not like these other fools,
They know that I stay true to who I am,
And they know I'm always there for my fam.
I do whatever the hell I want to do,
No longer doing what people tell me to.

You Wanna Be Me

I know people that want to be just like me,
but you don't want to open your eyes to see what I see.
You'd never last long living my life,
I'm just searching for my next ex-wife.
Love doesn't exist in this day and age,
but that notion no longer fills me with rage.
I've learnt to accept the ways of this crazy world,
and it no longer makes me want to hurl.
It's not my fault that people live f**ked up lives,
I do whatever I need to keep me happy while I survive.
I'll be joyful until I'm in the grave,
I know exactly how I'm supposed to behave.
I no longer live with any regrets,
but there's some things that I'll never forget.
I'll leave the devil to deal with all the bad,
coz I'll never meet him, I never went mad.
I'm not saying that what I have done wasn't absolutely crazy,
but trying to look back on it, it's all pretty hazy.
I'll never have to deal with that type of bulls**t again,
and once lost, you'll never again, become my friend.
Don't blame me for all of your imperfections,
and don't blame me when you receive the lethal injection.
It's not my fault that you're living the life that you chose,

and it's not my problem for what you're putting up your nose.
Back up away from me if you can't hold your own,
I can hold mine, and that's already been shown.
I don't care if you're green with envy,
I'm above you, I won't even consider you my enemy.

I'm Your Best Memory

I found myself when I was at the bottom of the pit,
when I had decided that I'd had enough of all of it.
So I picked myself up and I crawled all the way to the top,
and I will never quit, no matter how much I hear you say to stop.
I will always be at the top of my game,
and I'll make sure that everyone remembers my name.
I'm someone that always sticks in the memory,
maybe it's my charisma, or even the chemistry.
No matter what it is, I'm someone that you'll never forget.
Sorry though, I forgot your name, but I'll give you another chance, don't fret.
I don't remember you, unless you leave an impression on my brain,
It doesn't matter though if you're an intellectual, or just insane.
As long as you have something going for you,
and you know that what I say is true.
I'm only in this world for what I need,
I call it necessity, you may call it greed.
You'll never find another person like me,
even when lost through time, I'll be left inside your head, like another great memory...

Part 6
New Love

Beauty

Someone so beautiful,
So full of life.
Perfection, Indisputable,
Like clear moonlight

Your smile is so bright,
It would make the sun jealous.
Tender like a sprite,
That's so very zealous.

Gorgeous as the fields,
Of the highlands of Scotland.
Your strength could break shields,
Your beauty could rule islands.

You make me feel,
Like the first King.
My heart you steal,
But it is no sin.

I see a perfect soul,
Through flawless eyes.
Your love, more precious than gold,
My love for you, more vast than the skies

All I Ever Wanted

All I ever wanted was to be a part of your heart,
And for us to be together, to never be apart,
No one else in the world could ever compare,
Your smile to your soul, so perfect, so rare.

We have shared more than I thought we ever would,
I love you more than I ever thought I could.
I promise to give you all that I have to give,
I'll do anything for you as long as I live.

I hope that one day you will be able to realise,
Just how perfect you are when seen through my eyes

Part 7
The Trauma

Broken

Deep within my tortured soul,
In places where no demon goes,
Feeling weary, growing old,
Rotting in my personal gallows.

Blackened what was once gold.

Deep within my corrupted mind,
Surrounded by the Devils' lies,
Taking all that was mine,
A darker place you will not find.

Poisoned the concrete rose.

What Was

What was truth, what was lies?
Tongue of a snake with venomous eyes.
Always hiding in a secret disguise,
Samples of truth amongst treacherous lies.

Everything that you said, I believed,
I trusted you completely, but there was none for me.
How could you, continually deceive,
Always had plans, to get rid of me.

Treated like trash, thrown in the dirt,
Stomped on, just like a big fat turd.
Hit, abused, and you didn't trust me? That hurt.
Karma always remembers, and this time, your heart will be burnt.

I'm Tired

I'm tired of all the lies and deceit,
I'm sick of all your hypocrisy,
I'm surprised your lack of morals allows you to sleep,
Keep my name out of your mouth with the lies that you speak.
My frustration with your cheating is reaching its peak,
All I ever wanted was to find some peace,
But your trifling way keep coming to haunt me.

Caught Up

Caught up in her web of deceit and lies,
Looking back I should have seen it in her cold, dead eyes.
I'm sick of thinking about the what, how, who, when and whys,
I still feel love, but it's hiding in a disguise.
Nothing she can say or do now can take me by surprise,
Gonna play mumma with a new man who filled her belly with supplies.
More lies, more lies, leads me to despise.
Her, while she gets with more guys, more guys,
She says they give her butterflies.
So into herself she can't hear her son's cries, son's cries.
She's talking more s**t so it attracts more flies,
Spreading her legs for more guys between her thighs,
Being held down and getting sodomized.
Can't even change her ways because she doesn't even try.
Too greedy to look back and revise,
The destruction she causes when being selfish applies,
She sided with the devil when we lost good people to the skies,
Only caring for herself and hurting others, until the day she dies.

Truth

I have a lot of truth,
To say, with the freedom of speech,
Your tyranny of physical, emotional and mental abuse,
Is finished just like your credibility.
You will never treat my son badly again,
Throwing all care to the wind,
Abuse him again, and I'll be forced to kill for him.
Neglectful mother you don't even deserve the mother title,
Would rather your son end up in hospital, so you don't have to look after him,
Just to get drunk and have sex your priorities aren't right,
Willing to watch your son suffer so you can get high,
Meth, sex and booze is all you need in your life,
Ditch a three-year-old just to get some d**k inside.

In My Mind

Deep inside the mind,
where only I can see,
I can't seem to find,
the other part of me.
Floating in darkness,
is where my thoughts lie,
all throughout the starkness,
I can see myself die.

The end is getting near,
for this tired old soul,
yet, I have no fear,
for in death, there is no control.
Getting closer to the light,
I struggle to carry on,
to get past all the night,
and be a father to my son.

Part 8
Gypsy Girl Encounter

Gypsy Love

I'm not usually the type that's lost for words,
though now I don't know what to say and it's just absurd.
You came out of nowhere and you made me feel,
made me feel something that I didn't believe was real.
I never thought someone like you even existed.
Awoke things inside of me, no matter how much I resisted.
You told me that it was all or nothing',
I went all in, and now you're off running'.
Now it seems it's over before it really begun,
I guess it's time to go back to feeling numb.

It Was Over

It was over before it had begun,
Chasing stars but headed for the sun.
A fling with you, would be so destructive.
Something more meaningful, would be less disruptive.
I'm over all the games that you play,
That's why now, I won't see you on any day.

The Beast

You've unleashed the beast I fought so hard to kill,
You unlocked the cage and released him, he can't be concealed.
Opening your eyes, a whole new world is revealed,
From pain and misery to a life of wonder and expectation,
A life of received promises and adoration.
Receiving affection and being appreciated,
You awoke my world, my heart was reactivated.
Then you messed with my head, and I go agitated,
Now I'm moving on because I'm aware of the game,
I used to be a player, you're a playette, it's all the same.

Part 9
Back in The Trauma

The Cycle

Can't you see that since we got together that I've been dying inside?
Can't you see the life and light has been fading from my eyes?
You infected me with your poisons and left me to decay while you watch.
You enjoyed my torment, gladly looking on with your scotch.

I saw it all happening, I wasn't too blind to see,
I thought maybe I was wrong, I should have listened when my mind said "Flee".
There was never any you and me, it was just you controlling me.
Twice now you've made me your puppet, but just know there won't be a number three.

Final Thoughts

I can't believe how toxic you were to me and my son.
Who would have thought the worst person in his life would be his mum.
A narcissist that's full of lies and deceit,
you even admitted your willingness to cheat.
Stealing prohibited drugs to help you get through work,
you hated what you were doing but still put work first.
How can someone enjoy destroying others' will to live,
all you do is take, take, take, there's never any give.
You play the victim well because you're so good at deception,
I hope that karma gives you infection after infection.
Not telling the guys you sleep with that you have herpes.
Here's to hoping you keep catching STD's.
May all that you have done come back and bite you on the a**.
May it all come back to haunt you, real soon, real fast.